The History and Actuality of Imperialism

The History and Actuality of Imperialism

Rudolf Steiner

Frank Thomas Smith

Rudolf Steiner Publications

The History And Actuality Of Imperialism
(Revised Edition)
Copyright © 2020
by Rudolf Steiner Publications.
All Rights Reserved.

All rights reserved. No part of this book may be reproduced in any form or by any electronic or mechanical means including information storage and retrieval systems, without permission in writing from the author. The only exception is by a reviewer, who may quote short excerpts in a review.

Unabridged translation by Frank Thomas Smith
Edited and Revised by James D. Stewart
Cover designed by James D. Stewart

Visit the website at www.rsarchive.org

Printed in the United States of America

First Printing: July 2020

Rudolf Steiner Publications

ISBN-13: 978-1-948302-20-3 (print edition)
ISBN-13: 978-1-948302-21-0 (eBook edition)

CONTENTS

ABOUT THIS BOOK vi

1 Lecture 1 1

2 Lecture 2 15

3 Lecture 3 29

ABOUT THE AUTHOR 47
ABOUT THE TRANSLATOR 49
OTHER BOOKS BY FRANK THOMAS SMITH 51

ABOUT THIS BOOK

In 1920 Rudolf Steiner had already foreseen that the future imperialism would be economic rather than military or nationalistic. In these three lectures he describes the history of imperialism from ancient times to the present and into the future. The anglo-american would play an increasingly important role in future developments, so the English visitors who attended must have been especially attentive.

Lecture 1

The History and Actuality of Imperialism

Lecture 1
February 20, 1920

Today's lecture will be episodic, a kind of interspersion into our considerations, because I would like our English friends, who will soon be going home, to be able to take as much as possible with them. Therefore I will structure this lecture in a way to be as effective as possible. Today I would like, at first historically, not so much referring to the present — that can be done tomorrow perhaps — I would like to say something about imperialism, historically, but in a spiritual-scientific sense.

Imperialism is a much discussed phenomenon recently, and discussed by those who are more or less conscious of its relationship to the total phenomena of the present time. But when such things are discussed, what is not taken into account, or at least not enough, is that we live within the historical course of events, that we stand in a very definitive historical evolutionary epoch and that we can only understand this evolutionary epoch if we know where the phenomena which surround us, in which we live, come from.

Basically, what is most effective today and what will show itself to be an even more effective imperialism in the future will be its bearer — the Anglo-American people. As far as its name is concerned, it has shown itself to be something new: *economic imperialism*. But most important is the fact that everything said about this economic imperialism is untrue, everything, I would say, seems to be hanging in the air, which more or less consciously leads to untruthfulness. So in order to recognize how in these times realities are completely different from what is said about them, a more profound observation of the historical course of events is necessary.

I only need to mention one item of present-day phenomena in order to characterize the public's ability to judge. We have experienced how at first in various parts of Europe and finally even in Germany, Woodrow Wilson has been glorified. Our Swiss friends know very well that while Woodrow Wilson was being glorified I always spoke out against him in the sharpest terms here in Switzerland, for what Woodrow Wilson is today, he was of course also then when he was being glorified by the whole word. (It is already being reported — although I can't say if it's the complete truth — that in America they are thinking of declaring him unfit to govern, that there are doubts about his judgment.) The public's capacity for judgment, as it zips around the world today, is sufficiently characterized by such things.

And one must only remember a second thing. During the last four of five years, an enormous amount of pretty things have been talked about: the *self-determination of peoples* and so forth. All these things were not true, for what was behind them was something completely different, it was of course a question of power. And in order to understand what it's about, what is said, thought and judged, it is necessary to return to the realities. And when things such as imperialism are considered — "Imperial Federation League" is the official designation in England since the beginning of the twentieth century — we must realize that they are the recent products of an evolution and they go back to a remote past, and can only be explained by a true consideration of history.

We do not want to delve so deeply into the past as we could when studying the spiritual evolution of humanity, but we do want to go at least as far back as several centuries before the Christian era. We find imperialistic empires in Asia, and a subspecies of such empires in Egypt. Most characteristic of the Asiatic impulse are, for example, the historically known Persian empire and, especially, the Assyrian empire. But it is not sufficient to study this first phase of imperialism only in the last, historically known stage of the Assyrian empire, simply because the motivators dominating the Assyrian empire cannot be understood without reaching back to even earlier oriental conditions. Even in China, whose whole organization reaches so far back, the organization of recent times has changed so much that the true character of an oriental imperialism as it once existed is not recognized. However, the conditions which are known historically make it possible to see what the fundamentals are.

We cannot understand the old oriental imperialism without knowing the conscious relationship between people of a region, let's say an empire, and what we today would call the ruler or the rulers of that empire. Because of course our words for ruler or king and so forth no longer express the feelings about the ruler or the rulers. It is very difficult to understand the feelings of people in general of the third to fourth century before the Christian era because it is difficult nowadays to take account of how people felt in those ancient times about the relation of the physical world to the spiritual world. Today most people think, if they even think about a spiritual world, that it is somewhere in the distant beyond. And when the spiritual world is spoken about — and in the future it will again have to be spoken about as being present among us just as the sense world is — then what results is what has led for example to the Protestant mentality. But the essential nature of ancient times is that no distinction was made between the physical and spiritual worlds.

This is so much the case that when ancient times are referred to by people of today they can hardly imagine much consistency, for the way of thinking was so different then from what it is today. Rulers, a ruling caste, slaves, ruled people, that was reality — not something called a physical reality, but it was *the* reality, simultaneously the physical and the spiritual reality. And the ruler of an oriental empire — what was he? The ruler of the oriental empire was God. And for the people of those times there was no God beyond the clouds, no choir of spirits who surrounded the highest God — that view came later — but rather what we today call ministers or court jesters, somewhat disrespectfully, were beings of a divine nature. For it was obvious that because of the mystery schooling they had gone through, they had become something greater than ordinary people. They were looked up to, just as the Protestant mentality looks up to its God or certain more liberal circles look up to their invisible angels and such. Extra invisible angels or an extra super-sensible invisible God did not exist for the people of the ancient orient. Everything spiritual lived in man. In the common man lived a human soul. In those whom we would today call rulers, lived a divine soul, a God.

The concept of a really existing godly empire, which at the same time was a physical empire, is no longer taken into consideration. That a king has real divine power and dignity is considered absurd today, but was a reality in oriental imperialism.

As I mentioned, a subspecies was found in Egypt, for there we find a true transition to a later form. If we go back to the oldest form of imperialism, we find it based on the king being God who really physically appeared on earth, the son of heaven who physically appeared on earth, who was even the father of heaven. This is so paradoxical for the contemporary mind, that it seems unbelievable, but it is so. We can learn from Assyrian documents how conquests were justified. They were simply carried out. The justification was that they had to expand more and more the God's empire. When a territory was conquered and the inhabitants became subjects, then they had to worship the conqueror as their god. During those times no one thought of spreading a certain worldview. Why would it have been necessary? When the conquered people openly recognized the conqueror, followed him, then all was in order, they could believe whatever they wanted. Belief — personal opinion — wasn't touched in ancient times, nobody cared about it.

That was the first form in which imperialism appeared. The second form was when the ruler, the one who was to play a leading role, wasn't the god himself, but the god's envoy, or inspired by the god, interpenetrated with divinity.

The first imperialism is characterized by realities. When an oriental ruler of ancient times appeared before his people, it was in all his splendor, because as a god he was entitled to wear such clothes. It was the clothing of a god. That's what a god looked like. It meant nothing more than what the ruler wore was the fashion of the gods. And his paladins were not mere bureaucrats, but higher beings who accompanied him and did what they did with the power of higher beings.

Then came the time, as already mentioned, when the ruler and his paladins appeared as God's envoys, as interpenetrated with divinity, as representatives. That is very clear in Dionysus the Areopagite.

Read his writings, where he describes the complete hierarchy, from the deacons, archdeacons, bishops, archbishops, up to the church's whole hierarchy. How does he do this? Dionysus the Areopagite presents it as though in this earthly churchly hierarchy is mirrored what God is with his archangels and angles, supersensibly of course. So above we have the heavenly hierarchy and below its mirror image, the worldly hierarchy. The people of the worldly hierarchy, the deacons, archdeacons, wear certain clothes, and they perform their rituals; they are symbols. The first phase was characterized by realities, the second phase was characterized by signs, by symbols. But this has been more or less forgotten. Even Catholics understand little of the fact that the deacons, priests, bishops, archbishops are the representatives of the heavenly hierarchies. This has been mostly forgotten.

With the advancement of imperialism a division occurred, a real division. On one hand there were the leaders tending more towards being divine representatives, priestly, where the priests were kings; on the other hand the tendency towards the secular, although still by the grace of God. Basically these were the two forms: the churches and the empires.

During the first imperialism, when all was physical reality, something like this would have been unthinkable. But in the second phase of imperialism the division occurred. On one side more secular, but nevertheless representative of God, on the other side more church oriented, also representative of God. That system held until the middle ages and, I would even say, until the year 1806, but more as a shadow, retained in kings and paladins as God's representatives. The Roman Catholic Church's propagation tended more towards the priestly. But where this phenomenon of God's representative or envoy, which held through the entire middle ages, was most strongly maintained was in the so-called Holy Roman Empire of the German Nation, which finally disappeared in 1806. In "Holy" you have a whiff of what was divine during the ancient times on earth; "Roman" indicates the provenance, where it came from; "German Nation" was what it covered, the more secular element.

Therefore in the second phase of imperialism we no longer merely have the Church's anointed imperialism, but we have the tangled web of the divine and the secular anointed in the empires. That already began in the old Roman Empire during pre-Christian times and extended into the late Middle Ages. But this imperial Holy Roman Empire of the German Nation always had a double character. Remember that it goes back to Karl the Great [Charlemagne]. But Karl the Great was crowned by the Pope in Rome. http://en.wikipedia.org/wiki/Charlemagne. Therewith royal dignity became a symbol, so that what existed here on the physical earth was no longer reality. The people of the Middle Ages did not worship Karl the Great and Otto I as gods, which was the case in more ancient times, but they saw in them godly representatives. And that had to be continually confirmed, for of course it became ever weaker in consciousness. But it still retained a symbolic reality, a reality of signs. These emperors of the Holy Roman Empire of the German Nation went to Rome in order for the Pope to crown them. Istwan I was also crowned king of Hungary by the Pope in the year 1000. The anointment, and therefore the power, was bestowed on the world's rulers by the clergy.

It was also thought that there was justification for other people's being incorporated into the empire. Even Dante thought that the emperor of the Holy Roman Empire was justified in ruling the whole world. So the formula for imperialism is even to be found in Dante.

In fables and other lore where the events of history are crystallized in human consciousness, things are expressed from various viewpoints, not just one. We could say that in the eleventh and twelfth centuries in Europe the consciousness existed — not a clear one, more like a feeling — that once in ancient times in the Orient men lived on the physical earth who were themselves gods. They didn't think it was a superstition, oh no, rather they thought that such gods could no longer live on the earth because the earth had become so bad. That's been lost, what made men gods, the "Holy Grail" has been lost and now, in Central Europe, it can only be found in the way Percival found it: one seeks the way to find god within, whereas earlier god was a reality in the empire. Now the empire is merely a sum of symbols, of signs, and one must find the spirit in the symbols.

Of all the things which once existed, only remnants remain. Reality is deadened. Remnants remain, remnants of the most diverse kind. Generally, as long as things are real, definite, they later become ambiguous. And thus in Europe diversity grew from clear reality. As long as the Holy Roman Empire had meaning in human consciousness, the representative of the empire was powerful and competent enough to subdue the individual angel-symbols, the local princes, for that consciousness included the emperor's right to do so. But his right rested more or less on something ideal, which more and more lost its meaning, and the local princes remained. So we have in the Holy Roman Empire something which gradually had its inner substance squeezed out until only the exterior remained. The consciousness that earthly men were representatives of God was lost. And the expression for the fact that people no longer believed that certain individuals were representatives of God is Protestantism — protest against the idea of men as representatives of God.

If the principle of Protestantism had rigorously penetrated, no prince could have been crowned "by the Grace of God" again. But such things remained as remnants. These remnants remained until 1918, then they disappeared. These remnants, which had already lost all inner meaning, remained as outer appearances until then. The local German princes were the outer appearances; they only had meaning in those ancient times when they were symbols for an inspirational kingdom of heaven.

Other remnants remained. Not so long ago a pastoral letter was written by a Central-European bishop — perhaps he was an Archbishop. In that pastoral letter he more or less claimed that the catholic priest is more powerful than Jesus Christ for the simple reason that when the Catholic priest performs the transubstantiation at the altar, Jesus Christ must be present in the Sanctissimum, in the Host. The transubstantiation *must* really take place through the priest's power. It means that the action performed by the priest forces the Christ Jesus to be present on the altar. Therefore the more powerful is not the Christ Jesus, but he who performs the transubstantiation at the altar!

If we wish to understand such a thing which, as I said, appeared in a pastoral letter a few years ago, we must go back, not to the times of the second imperialism, but to the times of the first imperialism, many elements of which are retained in the Catholic Church and its institutions. Therein lies the remnant of the consciousness that those who rule on the earth are the gods, whereas the Christ Jesus is only the son of God. What was written in that pastoral letter is of course an impossibility for the Protestant mentality, just as for today it is almost impossible to believe that thousands of years ago people actually saw the ruler as God. But these are all real historical factors, real facts which played a role historically and are still present today.

This earlier realities play strongly into later events. Just look at how Mohammedanism [Islam] has spread. Certainly Mohammed never said: Mohammed is your God — as it would have been said thousands of yours earlier by an oriental ruler. He limited himself to what corresponded more to the times: There is a God, and Mohammed is his prophet. In people's consciousness he was God's representative — the second phase of imperialism. The manner in which Islam spread, however, corresponded to the first phase. For Muslims have never been intolerant towards other beliefs the way some others were. The Muslims were content to defeat the others and make them their subjects, just as it was in older times when a profession of faith was not required, for it was a matter of indifference what they believed if they just recognized God.

And something also remained of the first phase of imperialism — strongly influenced by the second — in Russian despotism, in tsarism. The way in which he was recognized by his subjects goes back, at least partially, to the first phase of imperialism. It was not so much a question of what was in the consciousness of the Russian people, for the rulership of the tzars rested on the Germanic and the Mongolian elements rather than that of the Russian peasantry itself.

Now we come to the third phase of imperialism. It has been formulated since the beginning of the twentieth century, since Chamberlain and his people coined the expression "Imperial Federation League", but the causes go back to the second half of the seventeenth century, when that great upheaval occurred in England as a result of which everywhere in the west that the Anglo-American people lived, the king, who earlier had been God, then an anointed one, became a kind of mere shadow — one cannot say a decoration exactly, but rather something more tolerated than taken seriously.

The English speaking peoples bring other preconditions to what we may call the people's will, the voting system, than, say, the French — the Latin peoples in general. The Latin peoples, especially the French, certainly carried out the revolution of the eighteenth century, but the French people today are more royal than any other. To be royal doesn't only mean to have a king at the top. Naturally a person whose head has been cut off cannot run around; but the French as a people are royal, imperialistic, without having a king. It has to do with the mood of soul. This "all are one" feeling, the national consciousness, is a real remnant of the Louis IV mentality.

But the English-speaking peoples brought other preconditions to what we may call the people's will. And little by little this became what the elected parliaments decided, and thus the third form of imperialism developed, which was formulated by Chamberlain and others. But today we want to consider this third imperialism psychologically.

The first imperialism had realities: One person was the God for the mentality of the other people. His paladins were the gods who surrounded him, sub-gods. The second form of imperialism: What was on the earth was the sign, the symbol. God acted within men. Third form of imperialism: Just as the previous evolution was from realities to signs and symbols, now the development is from symbols to platitudes.

This is an objective description of the facts, without being emotionally tinged. Since the seventeenth century what has been called the will of the people in the public life of the Anglo-American peoples in the law books — of course categorized according to classes — is no more than empty platitudes. Between what is said and reality there is not even the relation which existed between the symbol and reality. So the psychological path is this: from reality to symbol and then to platitudes — to words which have been squeezed out, dried out, empty words. This is the reality of the third imperialism: squeezed out, empty words. And nobody imagines that they are divine, at least not where they originated.

Just think about the basis of that imperialism, the ruling elements of which are empty platitudes: during the first imperialism the kings, in the second imperialism the anointed, now the empty platitudes. From majority decisions of course nothing real results, only a dominant empty platitude. The reality remains hidden. And now we come to an important factor upon which reality is based: the colonization system. Colonization played an important role in the development of this third imperialism. The "Imperial Federation League" summarizes the means of spreading imperialism to the colonies. But how do the colonies become part of the empire? Think back on real cases. Adventurers who no longer rightly fit into the empire, who are a somewhat down at heel, go to the colonies, become rich, then spend their riches at home, but that doesn't make them respectable, they are still adventurers, bohemians. That's how the colonial empire is created. That is the reality behind the empty platitudes. But remnants remain. Just as symbols and empty platitudes remain as remnants of the original realities, or symbolic crowns on princes and tsars, also from the enterprises of the somewhat foul smelling colonists, realities remain. The adventurer's son is not so foul smelling, right? He already smells better. The grandson smells even better and a time comes when everything smells very good. The empty platitudes are now possessed by what smells good. The empty platitudes are now identified with the true reality. Now the state can spread its wings, it becomes the protector and everything has been made honest.

It is necessary to call things by their real names — although the names seldom describe the reality. It's necessary because only thus can we understand what tasks and what responsibilities confront humanity in these times. Only in this way is it possible to realize what a *fable convenue* so called history really is, meaning *that* history which is taught in the schools and universities. That history does not call things by their real names. On the contrary, its effect is that the names describe what is false.

What I have just described is something terrible, isn't it. But you see, it's a question of guiding the feelings towards responsibilities.

Let's now consider the other side. Let's consider such an ancient empire. In people's minds it was an earthly reality; the priest-king came from the mysteries. The second was no longer earthly reality, it was symbolic. It is a long way from the godly jewelry the rulers and their paladins in the ancient oriental empires wore and the "Roter Adler" [Red Eagle] medals hung around people's necks long afterward. But that's how things evolved. It went from reality to nothing, not even a sign or symbol, but basically the expression of the empty platitude. Finally this empty platitude system, which has spread from the west to the rest of the world, has penetrated public affairs. I have even met court councilors — who anyway have little counseling to do — but what about the *titular* court councilors? Just an empty platitude hung on certain people and everything remains as before.

Whereas in the first phase the physical reality was thought to be spiritual, in the future this physical reality may no longer be thought of as spiritual. Nevertheless, the spiritual must be present here in the physical world. That means that spiritual reality must exist alongside physical reality. The human being must move around here within the physical reality, and recognize a spiritual reality, must speak of it as something real, supersensible, invisible, but which exists, which must be established among us.

I have spoken about something quite terrible: about the platitude. But if the world had not become so platitude oriented, there would be no room for the introduction of a spiritual empire. Precisely because everything old has now become platitudes, a space has come into being in which the spiritual empire can enter. Especially in the west, in the Anglo-American world people will continue to speak in the usual terminology, things that come from the past. It will continue to roll on like a bowling ball. It will roll on in the words. You can find innumerable expressions especially in the west which have lost all meaning, but are still used. But not only in these expressions, but in everything described by the old words the empty platitude lives, in which there is no reality, for it has been squeezed out. That is where the spiritual, which has nothing of the old in it, can find room. The old must first become empty platitude, everything that continues to roll on in speech thrown overboard, and something completely new must enter, which can only propagate as a world of the spirit.

Only then can there be a kingdom of Christ on earth. For in that empire a reality must exist: "My kingdom is not of this world." In the kingdom of this world, in which the kingdom of Christ will propagate, there will exist much that had not became empty platitude. But in the western world, everything originating in ancient times is destined to become platitude. Yes, in the west, in the Anglo-American world, all human tradition will become platitude. Therefore the responsibility exists to fill the empty vessel with spirit, about which can be said: "This kingdom is not of this world!" That is the great responsibility. It's not important how something came about, but what we do with what has come about. That is the situation.

Tomorrow we will speak about what can be done, for under the surface, especially in the western countries, the secret societies are most active, trying to insert the second phase of imperialism into the third. For in the Anglo-American people you have two imperialisms pushed together, the economic one of a Chamberlain and the symbolic imperialism of the secret societies, which play a very effective role, but which are kept secret from the people.

Lecture 2

The History and Actuality of Imperialism

Lecture 2

February 21, 1920

I have spoken to you about the historical origin of what today may be called imperialism, and you will have already noticed from what I said yesterday that it is essential to see how contemporary occurrences, which were once real factors in social life, are now merely leftovers from older times as far as reality is concerned. In olden times institutions and customs had their real meaning. To a certain extent they were realities. Realty has ended though. After passing through the stage of symbols, it has finally become a platitude.

In general we live in the age of platitudes. It is necessary, however, to realize that platitudes need a certain soil from which to grow, and on the other hand they are a preparation for something which is yet to come in human evolution. If the old realities had not transformed themselves into platitudes, that is, into something existing yet illusional, then the new reality could not come into being. The new could not come if for example a visible god appeared in human form as happened in the last years of the Roman empire. For the Roman emperors were, at least according to their pretensions, still gods. Nero, at least hypothetically, was a real god in human form. In the course of time such things have lost their meaning. They have passed through the stage of symbols and have become mere platitudes.

But the more things become platitudes, the more the terrain is prepared for a new reality — a spiritual life which is not derived from the sensible world, but from the supersensible world; for a spiritual life which does not seek the divine-spiritual beings in human form, but as real, genuine beings amongst the visible people on earth. First must come the age of platitudes which must, however, be recognized as such. Then the development of a new spiritual life will be possible. In order to understand the contemporary world under such disagreeable conditions, one must direct one's attention toward the birth of a new spiritual life, fully conscious of the illusionary nature of what was formerly reality in human evolution.

It is only natural that people want to hold on to the old realities, even when they have become platitudes; for to realize that they have become platitudes causes a feeling of insecurity. They feel that there is no longer solid ground under their feet if such things have become platitudes. People love to deceive themselves, and when the recognize the deception as deception, they feel that they are adrift. They will no longer feel themselves to be adrift when they can really feel the solidity of the new spiritual life. And we live in the age when we will have to be participants in the fall of the platitude stage and will have to be participants in the rise of the [new] spiritual life. And this will be especially possible if all English-speaking peoples realize that the traditions they have preserved from olden times and of which they still speak have become platitudes, and how the reality beneath these platitudes is the economy, as I explained yesterday.

But a moment will come, a moment which is very important. At the moment when it is recognized that we are dealing with an economic life which only becomes "reputable" in the third or fourth generation and otherwise with platitudes, as I also explained yesterday. At that moment we will recognize the inanity of the human being who merely participates in physical life as though it were the only reality. This knowledge must dawn especially on the peoples of the west. The moment of realization must come when we can no longer defend all that we maintained til now. Reality for us is what we do for our stomachs and digestion. As long as we have not seen through the platitudes and recognized them for what they are, as long as we do not realize that the economy is the only reality, we will not be able to admit what it is necessary to admit. If we do realize all that, then human nature can do no other than to say: in order to be human we need a spiritual reality in addition to the physical reality of the economy.

That moment of truth must dawn. Human evolution cannot advance further without this moment of truth. For the same reason that we go forward towards a new spiritual life, at present we must be immersed in the element of the platitude.

The peoples of the west have the greatest talent for this truth. All the prerequisites for the dawning of such truth is present in the peoples of the west, whereas the other European peoples have little disposition for such a truth to dawn on them with the necessary intensity. For them other conditions exist that prevent the illusions from being seen through so thoroughly, so radically, as they can be seen through by the English-speaking peoples. But once again we must keep the historical context in mind.

Consider for a moment that the various Central European tribes of Germanic origin were united since the time of Charlemagne's successors as the Holy Roman Empire, as I have already pointed out. That Holy Roman Empire was basically a network of pure symbols — all signs and symbols, which pointed to some kind of reality. It was not possible, however, to attain to full spiritual reality through the use of signs and symbols. The churches prevented it. Everything which the Middle Ages had to say about spiritual reality, and what the successors of the European confessions had to say about such a spiritual reality, had the character of the half-understood, the not-to-be-completely-understood. It had the character of colored light shining through the stained glass windows of the churches. The people recoiled when they approached the spiritual by means of the symbols; they recoiled in fear of a clear, sharp comprehension. On the contrary, they preferred to characterize the thing as being half unknown, which cannot be penetrated by knowledge.

It was also the case with social relationships. Studying the history of the Holy Roman Empire — and Swiss history is closely connected to it — we find that a lack of clarity was perpetuated from age to age. The lack of clarity in the social organism was perpetuated until finally in 1806 it became noticeable — even the Habsburgs realized it by then — that the Holy Roman Empire no longer made any sense. And the especially talented — that is negatively talented — Emperor Franz Joseph I abdicated the German crown. It lost the power to exist because no sense could be found behind the symbols. And the people of Central Europe were left with a striving in all directions, which contained but little concrete meaning.

Thus the founding of the Reich [empire] of 1870/71 with its inner contradictions. A German "empire" was created, but based on a false premise. The title "emperor" was invented. Perhaps in France under similar conditions the "empereur" would be understood, half-understood at least, because there was some substance left in the people; but in Germany a name existed which presumed that the people had a talent for mere names without meaning; that on one hand a talent for cultivating platitudes existed and on the other hand for the underlying reality of economic life. But that talent did not exist in Central Europe. And in order to understand what happened in Central Europe, history should not be studied based on abstract concepts, but on realities! We could ask the question: What happened in the German Reich between 1871 and 1914?

What people saw as happening from without was only an illusion. What was the reality? You see, with historical happenings something appears [draws on blackboard in red]; and beneath its surface something else appears [blue]. When the first thing disappears as an illusion, then the second thing, the reality, appears as its continuation. One should not analyze, but look for the concrete reality. What developed in the German Reich during 1871 to 1914 was not apparent then, for the Reich itself was an illusion. The reality came later, it is what has been happening since November 1918; it is those who are presently in power. The fundamental character of the Wilhelmian age is Gustav Noske [Minister of War]. The fundamental character of what had been developing for decades only became apparent when the present rulers appeared. The German ex-emperor is defined by the so-called revolutionary rulers of the present. The state of affairs which existed beneath the surface in the previous decades, during which illusions were cherished, is the state of affairs which exists today in reality.

You can really study history when you seek involution in evolution, in that you look for what is happening beneath the surface. What was Russian tsarism in the 19th century in reality? What Russian tsarism was then has appeared in its reality today: Lenin and Trotsky, Bolshevism. That is the concrete reality of what was then an illusion. Tsarism was the lie that floated on the surface; but what tsarism really cultivated appeared in its true reality after tsarism itself was swept away. Lenin was nothing other than the tsar; after the tsar has been skinned what remains today is the reality: Lenin or Trotsky. And, continuing this analogy, if you were to skin people like Caprivi or Hohenlohe or Bethman Hollweg [German Chancellors from 1890 through 1917], Moske and Scheidemann [German politician in office from 1903 to 1918] and so on remain. These are the real figures; the others were mere illusions.

It is a question of not illustrating historical phenomena with abstract concepts, but of showing the historical realities. In history the definition of one fact will always be another fact, not an abstract concept. Therefore it is a question of studying realities. For we are living in an age when realities must be closely observed and revealed.

This phenomenon is particularly obvious if you study the constitution, the content of the secret societies which possess great power in the English-speaking countries, a power unsuspected by the general public. They are societies organized outwardly under very sympathetic rules, and have become ever more powerful during the fifth post-Atlantean epoch.

If you look back to England in 1720, you will find very few members of these secret societies. Members are usually merely tools, the really powerful people stand behind them. But there were very few members. But if we look at the statistics today, we find 488 Masonic lodges in London. Such lodges are excellent tools in the hands of the secret societies. In Great Britain there are 1,354 lodges, in the colonies and overseas 486, and then 836 lodges in the world of the so-called Royal Arch Chapter, which keeps even the external Masonic rituals secret.

It is a matter of observing the substantial content of what actually exists within these lodges, for that is what is used as tools by the groups in power. And it is also important to discern why these powerful circles have been so meaningful even until today. The real content goes back to the far past. Those who keep claiming that the contents of Freemasonry go back to the far past are not so very wrong, although the things presented as examples are often nebulous, perhaps even quackery. They go so far back that we can say that the time they started was during the first stage of imperialism when the god walked around in human form. At that time the things spoken and especially the things shown in these lodges today made some sense. Then they became symbolic. The sense is long gone. One can say that what goes on in the lodges today has almost no content. Only the symbols remain.

The symbols continued into the stage of platitudes, so that we have, especially in the English-speaking areas and the other areas dependent upon them, two layers of cultural fermentation side by side: the external, exoteric platitudes of public life, and in the secret societies the symbols, which are only kept as tradition without any attempt to reach back to their original meanings. Thereby the symbols have become platitudes in symbolic form, or symbols which are also platitudes in a different form. You have therefore the external exoteric platitudes of public life, expressed in normal human language and which are extensively used in parliaments and congresses. Then you have the use of symbols in the secret societies, whose members usually don't understand them — platitudes in symbolic form. It is important that alongside the external purely literal platitudes we also have the cultural ceremonial platitudes. For these ceremonial platitudes at least contain spiritual elements. And in the secret societies which possess a real ceremonial form, meaning those which go back to the original practices, it can happen that through their karma certain especially talented people do get to the bottom of the symbols. And sometimes a blind chicken finds a kernel of corn. Sometimes especially talented people discover the meaning of the rituals; then they are expelled from the secret society. But care is taken that they can no longer be dangerous for the secret society. For what is especially important for these societies is power, not insight. It is important for them to keep the secrets in their original form. And they possess a certain power in this traditional form.

Why?

I have described for you the substantial content. But this content depends upon the people who are banded together in those societies. Just imagine how many people belong to the various lodges in the world. These people, when they enter the lodges, are confronted with the ceremonies, which are mannered as I described. But they are won for the lodges due to certain criteria. One of the most important criteria is the absolute indifference to the members' religious beliefs — although this criterion is sinned against in some cases. There are lodges, for example, which do not accept Jews. But they are ignorant of the basic principle, which is that people of all confessions are embraced, and individual beliefs are not touched. Also no attention is to be paid within the lodge to social class and other differences. In the correct lodges all are brothers, regardless of one being a lord and the other a worker — although this is also sinned against. Workers are not accepted in most lodges, only lords and others who are amenable to them. But that has nothing to do with the principle. Those who are within are totally united under the slogan: We are all brothers.

Then there are the degrees, which have nothing to do with the external social position of the members. The members are really united in a way which has nothing to do with their external social position. In our society people are divided firstly according to religion, whereas in the lodges the religions play no role. And secondly no one would claim that in the external social order men are all brothers. They are not brothers. In the lodges, however, those who belong to them are brothers.

Such things are really meaningful. It is not a matter of indifference under which viewpoints people come together in communities.

When people of the same confession come together in a community, then in real life it is often a community dedicated to external power — dead power. But when they come together under the viewpoint that the faith they profess is a matter of indifference, it becomes a community with particularly strong spiritual power. That is why the Catholic Church, wanting to keep people under a more or less unified faith, must always reinforce its power by political means. It has always been more powerful the less it has insisted on its creed, and less powerful the more it has insisted on creed; the less the hierarchy, Rome, has demanded adherence to creed. For in society in general to make religion the central issue results in lack of power. A community can only be powerful when it attaches no importance to individual beliefs.

This is a particularly important reality in the age of platitudes. For side by side with the public platitudes stand to some extent the esoteric platitudes of the ceremonies, of the rituals. This is the real reason for present day social confusion. One can cite some strange examples for the platitudinous nature of the times. You know that in the middle of the nineteenth century there were two opposing parties in the English parliament — the liberal Whigs and the conservative Tories. Whigs and Tories were in opposition. What kind of names were they? In the first half of the nineteenth century these names were seriously meant. The liberals were called Whigs, and no embarrassment was involved: the others were called Tories, also without embarrassment. But when these names were adopted during the dawn of the English parliament, what did they signify? The name Whigs was a cussword. When a Scottish group organized against a certain church discipline, in England they were called Whigs. And the platitude spread so far that a cussword became the group's official title. So the honorable Liberals acquired a name which was no longer a cussword. And the Tories — that name originated in Ireland. In the 17th, 18th century the papists were called Tories. Later that name, a cussword for Irish papists, became the official designation for the English conservatives. All this happened in the realm of names, in the realm of designations, in the realm of platitudes. Reality played no role here. This is of course superficial, but wherever you look you will find such things, first in the English speaking world, then in the rest of the world, to the extent it has been infected.

But what is it that brings so many men together in the lodges under such laudable viewpoints? It doesn't really matter that there are a small number of doubtful personages as well. The principles matter. It is very meaningful that all those people come together in ceremonial platitudes, which however keep them together on a real spiritual foundation.

It is true however, that when someone is a powerful minister, say, and needs an under-secretary of state, he naturally prefers a brother Mason to someone else. It is even justified, because he knows him better and can work better with him. This kind of cooperation is justified under the circumstances in which it arose, but must cease now.

But what does it mean? It is certainly remarkable that just in the age of platitudes which reign in public life a spiritual community appears with decidedly worthy principles. The spiritual community is quite secret, not so much as concerns its possessions, but rather its internal objectives. Why is this the case? Because we are living in the age of platitudes and platitudes encourage the falsification of realities. And what happens? What is basically already in existence? An independent economy which no longer coincides with the platitudes; a spiritual life driven underground and a rights life wrapped in a toga of platitudes, which has as much meaning for the external world as jurisprudence, as the English judge dressed in his judicial finery. Just to the extent this judicial finery corresponds to reality, jurisprudence corresponds to the reality behind the scenes. A triformation in the realm of the platitude, a triformation of the untruth, but proof for the necessity of the threefold society.

You see, to want the threefold society means to replace the lie and the platitude with the truth, but the truth as reality, whereas at the present time the period has begun in which reality is not truth, but platitude. Of course one can force platitudes into spiritual life as well as civil rights, the state; but that doesn't work well in the economy. Now comes something about which I always receive objections in many public lectures. After I explain how one can achieve insight into the spiritual world by following the indications in my book "How to Attain Knowledge of the Higher Worlds", after every third lecture someone stands up and says: "Yes, but how can one know that what he sees inwardly is real? There is such a thing as auto-suggestion. This whole spiritual world could by only an auto-suggestion! There is even the suggestion that when someone even thinks about lemonade he has a lemonade taste in the mouth." I always answer that it's a matter of standing in reality. Of course the taste of lemonade can be suggested, but your thirst cannot be quenched that way. If you go sufficiently far, you will reach reality. You can have platitudes in the realm of spirituality, even in the rights-state, but platitudes in the economy do not work because you can't eat them, or at least can't be filled by them.

So actually in the age of platitudes of all the realities the only one remaining is the economy. And in the moment that illusion is recognized as illusion, that the platitude is recognized as platitude, a strong feeling a shame will arise: We humans possess reason, but we only use this reason to insure the economic basis of physical life, something which animals do without possessing reason. If with our reason we do not achieve anything except to support the economy — food and the things necessary for physical existence, then we are prostituting our reason, then we are using our reason to accomplish something which the animal does quite well without the luxury of reason. In the moment that self-knowledge dawns, that is, when the platitudes are recognized for what they are, the feeling of shame arises; and then the reversal — the awareness of the necessity for renewal of spiritual/cultural life.

This must however be prepared in the correct way — that a sufficiently large number of people see through the contemporary situation. What good does it do if people only deceive themselves as to what is real. What good does it do to believe Lloyd George [British Prime Minster 1916-1922] when one sees through the fact that everything he says is necessarily platitude? What good does it do if the whole world worshiped Woodrow Wilson, when ones sees through the fact that Wilsonian politics were platitudes? What good does it do to dwell on European conditions today based on inherited principles from the past which are no longer valid?

Symbols should also be viewed in their historical context. It should be clear that outward appearances express remarkable things. The Habsburgs, for instance, came from Alsace and passed through Switzerland always moving east. They got as far east as they would go when they became the apostolic kings of Hungary. But in this journey from west to east, the remarkable thing is that the western realities faded away in the east.

The Hohenzollerns didn't take such a long journey — only from Nuremberg to Berlin, but also from west to east. These historical signs are also real symbols which we should pay attention to. And we should pay attention to the realities beneath the platitudes of today. That is why it is impossible to find reality in public opinion today. Whoever has a sense for reality arrives at some remarkable things. When you look into the origin of things in public life that everyone in the whole world is imitating, things like Whigs and Tories, you find that they were originally cusswords, and it was necessary to take them seriously because serious names for what really existed could not be found. And that's the situation with many things nowadays. In public life we try to enclose words in a kind of mystical shroud, and don't realize it. We don't realize that we are living in the age of platitudes.

For example I know of a very interesting codex consisting of a collection of platitudes. When you open this codex you find remarkable sentences. For example: What is justice? Justice is a people's will — and so on. Yes, my dear friends, The law is the will of a people! People — but today "people" is thought to be a mere sum of individuals. But this sum is supposed to have a will. That is the kind of explanation given in the codex of platitudes. One has the impression that someone wished to enjoy the luxury of translating into platitudes everything existing in public life today. And do you know the title of this codex of platitudes? *The State,* and its author is Woodrow Wilson. This codex appeared in the 1890s. Now it was not Woodrow Wilson's intention to enjoy the luxury of collecting all the platitudes in one book; nevertheless it was accomplished. So little had what people think and say to do with reality that in their opinion Woodrow Wilson had compiled the sum of today's political wisdom — but which was in reality a codex of platitudes. A few years ago the platitude bug bit a German so soundly that he translated this fat book into German. I assume that it will also be translated into other languages, but I don't know.

Without seeing through these things, without observing everywhere the realities in these things, we will not get far. One doesn't advance today with small thinking. It is necessary to motivate ourselves to think big. We will discuss this further tomorrow.

Lecture 3

The History and Actuality of Imperialism

Lecture 3
February 22, 1920

When you consider what has been said here during the past two days you will see that what belongs to the essence of imperialism is that in an imperialistic community something that was felt to be part of a mission — not necessarily justified, but understandable — later continued on as an automatism, so to speak. In the history of human development things are retained — simply due to indolence — which were once justified or explicable, but no longer are.

If a community is obliged to defend itself for a period of time, then it is surely justified to create certain professions for that purpose: police and military professions. But when the danger against which defense was necessary no longer exists, the professions continue to exist. The people involved must remain. They want to continue to exercise their professions and therefore we have something which is no longer justified by the circumstances. Something develops which, although perhaps originating due to the necessity for defense, takes on an aggressive character. It is so with all empires, except the original imperialism of the first human societies, of which I spoke yesterday, in which the people's mentality considered the ruler to be a god and thus justified in expanding his domain as far as possible. This justification was no longer there in all the subsequent empires.

Let us now consider once again from definite viewpoints what is apparent in the historical evolution of mankind. We find that in the oldest times the will of the individual who was seen as divine was the indisputable power factor. In public life there was in reality nothing to discuss in such empires; but this impossibility of discussion was grounded in the fact that a god in human form walked the earth as the ruler. That was, if I may say so, a secure foundation for public affairs.

Gradually all that which was based on divine will and was thus secure passed over to the second stage. In that stage the things which can be observed in physical life, be they persons, be they the persons' insignias, be they the deeds of the governing or ruling persons, it was all symbols, signs. Whereas during the first phase of imperialism here in the physical world the spirit was considered directly present, during the second stage everything physical was thought of as a reflection, as an image, as a symbol for what is not actually present in the physical world, but only illustrated by the persons and deeds in the physical world.

Such times, when the second stage appeared, was when it first occurred to people that a possibility for discussion of public affairs was possible. What we today call rights can hardly be considered as existing during the first stage. And the only political institution worth mentioning was the phenomenon of divine power exercised by physical people. In social affairs the only thing that mattered was the concrete will of a physical person. To try to judge whether this will was justified or not makes no sense. It was just there. It had to be obeyed.

To discuss whether the god in human form should or should not do this or that made no sense. In fact it was not done during those times when the conditions I have described really existed. But if one only saw an image of the spiritual world in physical institutions, if one spoke of what Saint Augustine called the "City of God" — that is, the state which exists here on earth, but which is really an image of heavenly facts and personalities, then one can hold the opinion that what the person does who is a divine image is right, is a true image: someone else could object and say that it is not a true image. That's when the possibility of discussion originated. The person of today, because he is accustomed to criticize everything, to discuss everything, thinks that to criticize and discuss was always present in human history. That is not true. Discussing and criticizing are attributes of the second stage, which I have described for you. Thus began the possibility to judge on one's own, that is, to add a predicate to a subject. In the oldest forms of human expression this personal judging was not at all present in respect to public affairs. During the second stage what we call today parliament for example was in preparation; for a parliament only makes sense when it is possible to discuss public affairs. Therefore, even the most primitive form of public discourse was a characteristic of the second stage. Today we live in the third stage, insofar as the characteristic form of the western countries more or less spreads over the world. This is the stage of platitudes. This stage of platitudes, as I characterized it to you yesterday, is the one in which the inner substance has also disappeared from discussion and therefore everyone can be right, or at least think that they are right, when it can't be proved that they are wrong, because basically within the world of platitudes everything can be affirmed. Nevertheless, previous stages are always retained within the next stages. Therefore the inner impulse to imperialism exists. People observe things very superficially. When the previous German

Kaiser wrote in a book that was opened out to write in: "The king's will is sublime law" — what did it mean? It meant that he expressed himself in the age of platitudes in a manner that only had meaning for the first stage. In the first stage it was really the case that the ruler's will was highest law. The concept of rights, which includes the right of free speech, and involves lawyers and courts, is essentially a characteristic of the second stage, and can only be grasped in its reality from the viewpoint of the second stage. Whoever has followed how much discussion has taken place about the origin and character of rights will have noticed that there is something shimmering in the rights concept as such, because it is applicable to the symbolic stage, where the spiritual shimmers through the material, shines, so that when only the external signs, the legal aspects and words appear, one can argue and discuss what are rights and the legal system in public discourse.

In the age of the platitudes, however, understanding of what is necessary for rights in society is completely lost: that the spiritual kingdom shines through into the physical kingdom. And then one arrives at such definitions as I described yesterday using the example of Woodrow Wilson. I will now read to you a definition of the law that Woodrow Wilson gave so you can see how this definition consists of nothing but platitudes. He said: "The law is the will of the state in respect to those citizens who are bound by it." So the state unfolds a will! One can well imagine that someone who is embedded so strongly in abstract idealism, not to mention materialism — for they are practically the same — can claim that the state is supposed to have a will. He would have to have lost all sense of reality to even conceive of such a thing let alone write it down. But it is in the book I spoke to you about yesterday — the codex of platitudes: *The State, Elements of Historical and Practical Politics*.

There are other interesting things in it. Only in parenthesis I would like to draw your attention to what Wilson says in this book about the German Empire after he describes how the efforts to found it were finally successful in 1870/71. He describes this with the following sentences: "The final incentive for achievement of complete national unity was brought about by the German-French war of 1870/71. Prussia's brilliant success in this struggle, fought in the interest of German patriotism against French impertinence, caused the cool restraint of the central states towards their powerful neighbor in the north to end; they united with the rest of Germany and the German Empire was founded in the royal palace at Versailles on January 18, 1871." The same man wrote that who a short time later in Versailles united with those whose impertinence had once been the motivation for the founding of the German Empire. Much of present day public opinion derives from the fact that people are so terribly superficial and pay no attention to the facts. If you decide to decide according to objective information, then things look quite different from what is propounded in public and accepted by thousands upon thousands of people. It wouldn't have hurt one bit if when Woodrow Wilson arrived in Paris in glory, praised from all sides, if these remarks had been held up to him. That is what must be striven for, to take the facts into account, which means also the truth.

So the second stage is when discussion arises, which is what makes the civil rights concept possible. The third stage is when economic life is the essential reality. And yesterday we showed how this [present] age of platitudes is absolutely necessary in the course of historical evolution in order that the platitude, which is empty, can open people's eyes to the fact that the only reality is economic life and how it is therefore so necessary to propagate spirituality, the new spirituality in the world.

People have quite a skimpy idea about this new spiritual life. And it is therefore understandable that it is burdened with the most ridiculous misunderstandings. For this new spirituality must penetrate into the depths of human life. And although those secret societies, about which I spoke yesterday, only traditionally preserve the old forms, the slogan "brothers", meaning not to let social class or an individual's religion play a part in the lodges, in a certain sense does prepare for it in the right way.

We say today — I beg you to pay special attention to this, let's take something quite banal, quite common: "The tree is green". This is a manner of speaking which is common to the second stage of human development. Perhaps you will understand me better if you imagine that we try to paint this opinion — that "the tree is green". You cannot paint it! There will be some white surface and green will be added, but nothing about the tree has been painted. And when something of the tree is painted which isn't green all you do is disturb the effect even more. If you try to paint "The tree is green", you are painting something dead. The way we combine subject and predicate in our speech is only useful for our view of the dead, of the non-living in the world. As we still have no idea of how everything in the world is alive, and how to express ourselves about what is alive, we form such judgments as "The tree is green", which presupposes that a relationship exists between something and the color green, whereas the color green is itself the creative element, the force which acts and lives. The transformation of human thinking and feeling will have to take place within the innermost life of the soul. This will take a long time to accomplish, but when it does it will affect social conditions and how people relate to each other.

Today we are only at the beginning of all this. But it is necessary to know which paths lead to the light. I have said that it is meaningful when people get together and each one's subjective beliefs play no role. And consider it from this viewpoint — really think about it — the way in which anthroposophy is described. It is not described through definitions or ordinary judgments. We try to create images, to present things from the most varied sides, and it is senseless to try and nail down something meant in a spiritual-scientific sense with a mere yes or no opinion. People today always want to do that, but it isn't possible. In happens ever more frequently — because we are growing out of the second stage and into the third — that someone asks: What is good for me in order to counter this or that difficulty in life? Advice is given. Aha! The person concerned says, so in this or that situation in life one must do this or that. They generalize. But it has only a limited meaning, for judgments given from the spiritual world always only have only an individual meaning, are only applicable to one case. This way of generalizing, which we have become accustomed to in the second stage, must not continue into the third stage. People today are very much inclined to carry things over from the past into the future. One can become disinclined towards the things which are pernicious for the soul by seeing clearly what is happening.

Yesterday I indicated to you that in many respects the Catholic Church harks back to the first stage. It contains something like a sham or a shadow of the first stage of human evolution, which sometimes solidifies into a kind of spiritual imperialism, as for example in the 11th century when the Monks of Cluny http://en.wikipedia.org/wiki/Cluny_Abbey really ruled over Europe more than is thought. From their ranks the powerful, imperialistic Pope Gregory VII emerged. Therefore Roman Catholic dogma enables the priest to feel greater than Christ, because he can force him to be present at the altar. This clearly shows that the institution of the Catholic Church is a relic, a shadow-image of what existed in the very first imperialism.

You know that a great enmity existed between the Catholic Church and the secret societies which used Freemasonry in the west — a certain form of Freemasonry at least — as their instrument. It would go too far in this lecture to describe in detail how this enmity has gradually increased over time. But one thing can be said, how in these secret societies the opinion is very strong that the Catholic Church is a relic of the first stage of imperialism.

The Holy Roman Empire used this framework to have Charlemagne and the Ottos crowned by the pope, thereby using the imperialism of the soul as the means of mundane anointment. They took what still remained from older times and poured it into the new. Thus the imperialism of the second stage was poured into the framework of the first imperialism.

Now we have arrived at the third stage, which shows itself to be economic imperialism, especially in the west. This economic imperialism is connected to a background culture of secret societies, which are sated with empty symbols. But while it has become clear that the social constitution of the Church is a shadow-image of what once existed and no longer has meaning, it is still not understood that in the second stage the statesmen of the west still suffer under a great illusion. Woodrow Wilson would no longer speak of the will of the Church, but he speaks of the will of the State as being self-evident.

But the state only had the importance attributed to it during the second stage of human development. Whereas during the oldest, the first stage the Church was all-powerful, in the second stage the state contains everything that was attributed to the Church in the first stage. Thus the economic imperialism of Great Britain and even a certain idea of freedom has been poured into the state. And those who were educated in Great Britain see in the state something that can well have a will of its own.

But we must perceive that this concept of the state must take the same road the concept of the Church has traveled. It must be realized: If we retain this concept of the state for the entire social organism, a mere rights institution, and force everything else into this rights institution, we are propagating a shadow just as the Church has propagated a shadow — recognized as such by the secret societies. There is little awareness of this though. Think of all the public affairs that people are enthusiastic about which are pressed into the concept of the political state. There are nationalists, chauvinists and so forth; everything we call nation, national, chauvinism, it's all incorporated into the framework of the state. Nationalism is added and the concept of the "nation-state" is construed. Or we may have a certain opinion about, say socialism, even radical socialism: the framework of the state is used. Instead of nationalism, socialism is incorporated. But then we have no concept; it can only be a shadow-image, as the constitution of the Church has become.

In some Protestant circles the idea has arisen that the Church is only the visible institution, that the essence of religion must take root in people's hearts. But this degree of human development has not yet arrived in respect to the political state, otherwise we wouldn't be trying to squeeze all kinds of nationalisms into the political boundaries which exist as the result of the war [First World War – trans.] All this neglects to take one thing into consideration — the fact that what occurs in the historical development of humanity is life and not mechanism. And a characteristic of life is that it comes and goes. The imperialistic approach is different however. According to this approach one does not think about the future. This is part of the present-day approach to public affairs, that people have no living thoughts, only dead ones. They think: Today we instituted something, it is good, therefore it must remain forever. The feminist movement thinks like this, as do the socialists and the nationalists.

We have founded something, it begins with us, everything waited for us until we became clever enough. And now we have discovered the cleverest that exists and it will continue to exist forever. It's as though I have brought up a child until he is eighteen years old and I say: I have brought him up correctly, and he will stay as he is. But he will get older, and he will also die, as does everything in the course of human evolution.

Now I come to what I mention before about what must accompany the principle of indifference to one's religious beliefs and fraternity. What must accompany them is the awareness that life on earth includes death and that we are aware that the institutions we create must of necessity also cease to exist, because the death principle already resides in them and they therefore have no wish to exist forever, do not consider being permanent. Of course under the influence of the thinking characteristic of the second stage this is not possible . But if the feeling of shame of which I spoke yesterday arises, when we realize that we are living in the kingdom of platitudes under which only economic imperialism glimmers — then will we call for the spirit, invisible but real. We will call for a knowledge of the spirit, one which speaks of an invisible kingdom, a kingdom which is not of this world in which the Christ-impulse can actually gain a foothold.

This can only happen when the social order is tripartite, threefold: The economy is auto-administered, the political state is no longer the absolute, all-inclusive entity, but is exclusively concerned with rights alone, and spiritual/cultural life is truly free, meaning that here in reality a free spiritual sector can be organized. The spiritual life of humanity can only be free if it is dependent only upon itself and when all the institutions responsible for cultivating the spirit, that is, cultural life, are dependent only upon themselves.

What do we have then, when we have this tripartite organism, this social organism? We have an economy in which the living physical earth is predominant. In this sector the economic forces of the economy itself are active. I doubt anyone will think that if the economy is organized as described in my book Towards Social Renewal — Basic Issues of the Social Question some kind of super-sensible forces will be present. When we eat, when we prepare out food, when we make our clothing, it is all reality. Esthetics may be symbolically present, but the actual clothing is the reality.

When we look at the second sector of the future social organism [the rights sector], we don't a symbolism like the second stage, where the political state constituted the totality, but we have what is valid for one person being equally valid for the other.

And the third sector will be neither symbol nor platitude, but a spiritual/cultural reality.

The spirit will possess the possibility of really living within humanity.

The inner social order can only be built through a transition to inner truthfulness. In the age of platitudes this will be especially difficult though. For during the age of platitudes people acquire a certain ingenious cleverness, which is, however, nothing more than a play on words of the old concepts. Just consider for a moment a characteristic example. Suddenly from the imperialism of platitudes comes the idea that it would be good if the queen of England also has the title "Empress of India". One can invent the most beautiful reasons for this, but if it didn't happen, nothing would have changed. The Emperor of Austria, who now belongs to the deposed royalty, before he was chased out carried around along with his other titles a most unusual one: Franz Joseph I, Emperor of Austria,

Apostolic King of Hungary, King of Bohemia, Dalmatia, Croatia, Slovenia, Galizia, Lodomeria, Illyia and so on. Among all these titles was also "King of Jerusalem"! The Austrian Emperor also carried, until he was no longer emperor, the title "King of Jerusalem". It came from the crusades. It would be impossible to give a better example of meaninglessness than this. And such meaninglessness plays a much greater role than you imagine. It a question of whether we can arise to a recognition of the present-day platitudes. It is made difficult because those who live in platitudes are the verbal representatives of the old concepts that stagger around in their brains imitating thoughts. But one can only achieve real thinking again when the inner soul-life is filled with substance and that can only come from knowledge of the spiritual world, of spiritual life. Only by being relieved by the spirit can one become a complete person, after having been constipated with platitudes.

What I described yesterday as a feeling of shame will result in the call for the spirit. And the propagation of the spirit will only be possible if the spiritual/cultural sector is allowed to develop independently. Otherwise we will always have to take advantage of loopholes, as was the case with the Waldorf School because the Württemberg Province education law had such a loophole which made it possible to establish a Waldorf school only according spiritual laws, according to spiritual principles, something which in practically no only place on earth would be possible. But one can only organize the things concerning the spiritual life from the spirit itself if the other two sectors do not interfere, if everything is taken directly from the spiritual sector itself.

At present the tendency is the reverse. But this tendency does not reckon with the fact that with every new generation a new spiritual/cultural life appears on earth. It's immaterial whether a dictatorship or a republic is established, if it is not understood that everything which appears is subject to life and must be continuously transformed, must pass through death and be formed anew, pass through metamorphoses, then all that will be accomplished is that every new generation will be revolutionary. Because only what is considered good for the present will be established. A fundamental concept for the western areas which are so mired in platitudes must be to see the social organism as something living. And one sees it as living only when it is considered in its threefold nature. It is just those whose favorable economic position allows them to spread an [economic] imperialism over practically the whole world who have the terrible responsibility of recognizing that the cultivation of a true spiritual life must be poured into this imperialism. It is ironic that an economic empire which spread over the whole world was founded on the British Isles and then when they were seeking mystical spirituality turned to those whom they had economically conquered and exploited. [India – Tr.] The obligation exists to allow one's own spiritual substance to flow into the social organism.

That is the awareness which our British friends should take with them, that now, in this worldwide important historic moment, in all the world's economic institutions where English is spoken, the responsibility exists to introduce true spirituality into the exterior economic empire. It's an either/or situation: Either efforts remain exclusively oriented towards the economy — in which case the fall of earthly civilization is the inevitable result — or spirit will be poured into this economic empire, in which case what was intended for earthly evolution will be achieved. I would like to say: Every morning we should bear this in mind very seriously and all activities should be organized according to this impulse. The bell tolls with extreme urgency at present — with terrible urgency. In a certain sense we have reached the climax of platitudes. In an age when all content has been squeezed out of platitudes, content which came to humanity previously but which no longer has any meaning, we must absorb real substantial content into our psychological and social life. We must be clear about the fact that this either/or must be decided by each individual for him or herself and that each must participate in this decision with his most inner force of soul.

Otherwise he does not participate in the affairs of humanity.

But the attraction for illusion is especially strong in the age of platitudes. We wish so to sweep away the seriousness of life. We avoid looking at the truth inherent in our evolution. How could people let themselves be deceived by Wilsonian ideas if they really had the intense desire for truthful clarity? It must come. The desire for truth must grow in humanity. Above all, the desire for the liberation of spiritual/cultural life must grow along with the knowledge that nobody has the right to call himself a Christian who has not grasped the saying: "My kingdom is not of this world."

This means that the kingdom of Christ must become an invisible kingdom, a truly invisible empire, an empire of which one speaks as of invisible things. Only when spiritual science gains in importance will people speak of this empire. Not some church, not some state, not some economic empire can create this empire. Only the will of the individual who lives in a liberated spiritual/cultural life can create this empire.

It is difficult to believe that in the lands in which people are downtrodden much can be done to free spiritual life. Therefore it must be done in those lands where the people are not downtrodden politically, economically and, obviously, not spiritually downtrodden. Above all it must be realized that we have not arrived at the day when we say: Until now things have gone downhill, they will go uphill again! No, if people do not act for this objective out of the spirit, things will not go uphill again, but will continue downhill. Humanity does not live today from what it has produced — for to produce again a spiritual impulse is necessary — humanity lives today from reserves, from old reserves, and they are being used up.

And it is childish and naïve to think that a low point is reached some day and things will get better then, even with our hands in our laps. That's not how it is. And I would like to see that the words spoken here kindle a fire in the hearts of those who belong to the anthroposophical movement. I would hope that the specter which perhaps haunts those who find their way to this anthroposophical movement be overcome by the spirit meant here. It is certainly true that someone who finds his way to such a movement often seeks something for himself, for his soul. Of course he can have that, but only in order to stand with his soul in the service of the whole. He should advance, certainly, for himself, but only so mankind can advance through him. I cannot say that often enough. It should be added to those things I said should be thought about every morning.

If we had really taken the inner impulse of this movement seriously, we would have been much farther along. But perhaps what is done in our circles does not help advance towards the future, but is often a hindrance. We should ask ourselves why this is so. It is very important. And above all we should not think that the sharpest powers of opposition are not active from all sides against what strives for the well-being of humanity. I have already indicated to you what is being done in the world in opposition to our movement, what hostility is activated against us. I feel myself obliged to make these things known to you, so that you should never say to yourself: We have already refuted this or that. We have refuted nothing, because these opponents are not interested in the truth. They prefer to ignore as much as possible the facts and simply aim slanderous accusations from all corners.

I would like to read part of a letter to you which arrived recently from Oslo. "One of our anthroposophical friends works in a socalled people's college in Oslo together with a certain Shirmer. This Mr. Shirmer is in a certain sense quite a proficient teacher, but is also a fanatical racist and a sworn anti-Semite. At a people's meeting where three of us gave lectures about the Threefold Society, he talked against us, or rather against Dr. Steiner's Towards Social Renewal, although without much success. The guy has a certain influence in teachers' circles and he works in his own way in the sense of the social triformation in the school insofar as he is for freedom, but on the other hand he works against the social triformation and Dr Steiner for the simple reason that he suspects that Dr Steiner is a Jew. That is perhaps not so bad. We must expect and overcome more serious opposition. But now he has received confirmation of his suspicion. He turned to an "authority", namely the editor of the political anthropological monthly, Berlin-Stiglitz. This purely anti-Semitic magazine wrote to him that Dr. Steiner is a Jew through and through. He is associated with the Zionists. And the editor added that they, the anti-Semites, have had their eye on you [Dr Steiner] for a long time. Mr Schirmer also says that a persecution of the Jews is beginning now in Germany, and that all the Jews on the anti-Semites' blacklist should be simply shot down or, as they say, rendered harmless." and so on.

You see, this has nothing to do with antisemitism as such, that's only on the face of it. They choose slogans in these situations, with which they try to accomplish as much as possible with people who listen to slogans. But such things clearly indicate what most people don't want to see, what they want to ignore more and more. It is today much more serious that you think, and we should not ignore the seriousness of the times, but should realize that we are only at the beginning of these things which are opposed to everything that is intended to advance human progress. And that we should never, without neglecting our responsibilities, divert our attention from what is a radical evil within humanity, what manifests as a radical evil within humanity. The worst that can happen today is paying attention to mere slogans and platitudes, and believing that outdated concepts somehow have roots in human reality today — if we do not initiate a new reality from the sources of the spirit itself.

That, my dear friends, was what I wanted to tell you today, first of all to all of you, but especially to those whose visit has pleased us greatly — especially to our English friends, so that when they return to their own country, where it will be so important, they will have something on which to base their activities. You will have seen that I have not spoken in favor or against anyone, nor have I flattered anyone. I only speak here in order to say the truth. I have known theosophists who when they speak to members of a foreign nation begin to talk about what an honor it is to be able to spread the teachings about the spiritual life in a nation which has accumulated so much glory. Such things cannot be said to you here. But I believe that you have come here to hear the truth and I think that I have best served you by really trying to tell the unvarnished truth. You will have learned during your trip that telling the truth nowadays is not a comfortable thing, for the truth calls forth opposition now more than ever. Do not be afraid of opposition, for they are one and the same: to have enemies and to tell the truth. And we will understand each other best when our mutual understanding is based on the desire to hear the unvarnished truth.

Before I leave for Germany, this is what I wanted to say to you today, and especially to our English friends.

RUDOLF STEINER

ABOUT THE AUTHOR

Born in Austria in 1861, Rudolf Steiner received recognition as a scholar when he was invited to edit the Kürschner edition of the natural scientific writings of Goethe. In 1891, Steiner received his Ph.D. at the University of Rostock. He then began his work as a lecturer. From the turn of the century to his death in 1925, he delivered well over 6700 lectures. His written works eventually included some fifty titles.

The philosophical outlook of Rudolf Steiner embraces such fundamental questions as the being of man, the nature and purpose of freedom, the meaning of evolution, the relation of man to nature, the life after death and before birth. Through a study of his writings, one can come to a dear, reasonable, comprehensive understanding of the human being and his place in the universe.

Among the activities springing from the work of Rudolf Steiner are the Bio-Dynamic Farming and Gardening Association which aims at improved nutrition resulting from methods of agriculture outlined by Rudolf Steiner; the art of Eurythmy, created and described by him as "visible speech and visible song;" the work of the Clinical and Therapeutical Institute of Arlesheim, Switzerland, with related institutions in other countries; the homes for the treatment of mentally retarded children; and new directions of work in such fields as Mathematics, Physics, Painting, Sculpture, Music

Therapy, Drama, Speech Formation, Astronomy, Economics and Psychology.

The success of Rudolf Steiner Education (sometimes referred to as Waldorf Education) has proven the correctness of Steiner's concept of the way to prepare the child for his eventual adult role in and his contribution to modern society. Today there are some seventy Rudolf Steiner Schools in existence in seventeen countries including the United States, Canada, Mexico, and South America, with hundreds of thousands of children enrolled.

ABOUT THE TRANSLATOR

Frank Thomas Smith

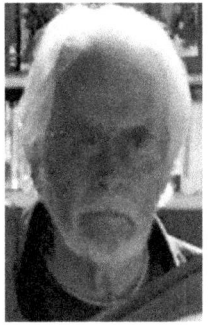

Frank Thomas Smith is an American expatriot who has lived most of his life in Europe (Switzerland and Germany) and South America (Argentina). During his career in the airline industry, he moonlighted in education (Waldorf), translating and writing — including children's fiction. What was once moonlighting is now full-time. He lives on a mountain in Argentina.

OTHER BOOKS BY FRANK THOMAS SMITH

Toward a Threefold Society

This work, written late in the life of Rudolf Steiner, makes use of a threefold analysis of the human individual and of human society. Man as an individual, or in a group, functions basically in three modes: thinking/perceiving, feeling/valuing, and willing/planning/acting. A unit of functioning, whether a part of an individual or part of a society has its proper role. Each role needs a certain respect from other areas if it is to function properly. Each role should be appropriately related to the other two roles or functions. In society, the three partitions are: the cultural-spiritual, the production-economic, and the "sphere of rights" including legal rights. As the analysis unfolds, it may be noticed that there is seldom a "pure case" but there are various mixes with one aspect often predominating. The manner in which the three aspects of society relate to the three aspects of the individual is a fascinating and intricate one, and one which has an important bearing on the future of human society.

OTHER BOOKS BY FRANK THOMAS SMITH

Anthroposophical Fantasies

Anthroposophy, also known as Spiritual Science, is not known for fantastic literature, or fiction at all. So how can stories with titles like "Life on Mars," or "The Girl in the Floppy Hat," or "To Hunt a Nazi" qualify as anthroposophical. They do not — until now. Therefore, this book is groundbreaking. You may smile at times, even laugh; other stories may cause a lump in your throat, perhaps even a tear or two. Oh, and by the way, fundamentalists are advised not to partake of this fantastical frosting on their anthroposophical cake. Here, then, are thirteen provocative, groundbreaking fictional tales for anthroposophists, and really anyone, to enjoy. By Roberto Fox, as told to Frank Thomas Smith.

www.ingramcontent.com/pod-product-compliance
Lightning Source LLC
Chambersburg PA
CBHW052125110526
44592CB00013B/1751